DISTANT   RELATIONS

DISTANT RELATIONS

CHERYL WHITEHEAD

LOBLOLLY
PRESS
ASHEVILLE, NC

LOBLOLLY PRESS
Asheville, NC

Copyright © 2025 by Cheryl Whitehead

All rights reserved. No part of this publication may be reproduced, distributed, or transmitted in any form by any means, including photocopying, recording, or other electronic methods without the prior written permission of the author, except in the case of brief quotations embodied in reviews and certain other noncommercial uses permitted by copyright law. For permission requests, write to the publisher at loblolly.publishing@gmail.com.

From MEMORIAL: A VERSION OF HOMER'S ILIAD by Alice Oswald
Copyright © 2011 by Alice Oswald. Used by permission of W. W. Norton & Company, Inc.

This is a work of fiction. Names, characters, places, and incidents either are the product of the author's imagination or are used fictitiously, and any resemblance to actual persons, living or dead, businesses, companies, events, or locales is entirely coincidental.

Book design by Andrew Mack
Author and cover photograph by Garrison Mack
Cover design by Emma Ensley

Published by Loblolly Press
loblollypress.com
Instagram: @loblolly_press

ISBN: 979-8-9900730-3-6
Printed in the United States of America
Library of Congress Control Number: 2024951037

First Printing, April 2024

Like leaves who could write a history of leaves
The wind blows their ghosts to the ground
And the spring breathes new leaf into the woods
Thousands of names thousands of leaves
When you remember them remember this
Dead bodies are their lineage
Which matter no more than the leaves

—**ALICE OSWALD,** MEMORIAL

CONTENTS

I

3	FARM FRAGMENTS
5	SELF PORTRAIT WITH LEAVES
6	DEPARTED PASSING THROUGH
7	CURIOUS FACT
8	LANDSCAPE WITH FOG
10	FLOCK OF SWALLOWS
11	UNKEMPT PASTURE
12	OCTOBER BEANS
13	CLOSER TO THE GROUND
14	ADOLPHUS' SCYTHE
15	LITTLE SUMMER
16	BAND OF TAMBOURINES
17	BROTHER BEEKEEPER
18	WAKE
19	UNEXPECTED ATTRACTION

II

23	FAMILY PORTRAIT
25	A HISTORY OF WIND
26	WEATHER & JUG BAND
27	DEBRIS
28	LAMP WICK
29	AMERICAN SENTENCES
30	LANDSCAPE WITH RUINS
31	TRACKS IN GRASS
32	WEATHER REPORT
33	BODY DOUBLE
34	LANDSCAPE WITH TIME

III

37	DISTANT RELATIONS
38	THUNDER
39	PALE LIGHT
40	ASSEMBLAGES
41	CHICKEN HOUSES
42	CLIMBING HYDRANGEA
43	AGING FATHER
44	LANDSCAPE OF THE SPANGLED MIND

IV

47	MIDDLE DISTANCE
48	INSTRUCTIONS FOR WINTER
49	ON PEERING THROUGH DECEMBER WINDOWS
50	IN HIS MIND HE VIEWS A BLIZZARD
51	PLOWMAN'S CHAPEL
52	NOCTURNE
53	A CERTAIN NOSTALGIA
54	SHADOWS KEEP HOUSE
55	GOD IS PLENTY

DISTANT   RELATIONS

I

FARM FRAGMENTS

Stillborn rabbit curled in clover.
Red specks on her belly.

*

Eyesore near the stop sign:
an unoccupied single wide.

*

Two red chicken houses on the ridge.
The wood frame of a third.

*

Sawdust glitters in the tufted tails
of six fox kits.

*

Knee-deep dandelions.
Faded newspaper in a gravel drive.

*

In the waterlogged culvert,
a croaking chorus.

*

Near Crutchfield's Crossroads, a hawk
spooks two heifers in the pasture.

*

Purple thistles twist in the ditch.
Goldfinches feast in green.

*

Two black & white mutts meander
near a mound of golden cantaloupes.

*

A cap dangles on a porch nail.
The sweat-scent lingers.

*

A Kelvinator & cast-iron stove
rust on a screened-in front porch.

*

Spider webs in the well house.
Rope crank & rusty bucket.

SELF PORTRAIT WITH LEAVES

To slip across the road
with the scrape of a dead leaf
& never be seen. A wind-blown
rope strikes the gate's frame

        clanging an orchestra's A.
        In the side yard, wild onions
        forget the rain & leaves
        heaped on a lean-to's roof.

Every abandoned farmhouse
with leaves drifting
into the chimney's mouth,
whispers of collapse.

        Light perceives the rift
        between winter & leaves
        & begins a treatise on harmony.
        O grim shirttail.

O tattered leaves
& pond of shimmering algae.
O hoof raised at an angle
before sloshing in mud.

DEPARTED PASSING THROUGH

after Mark Jarman

My father returns as a field of tender
radishes in snow, bright green stems
& leaves holding on in white furrows,

as a plow in the barn, & the dappled horse
shivering in the pasture. He returns
as snowmelt over-running a ditch,

turning a low place into a river
flooding the cemetery. He's
steam billowing from dry kilns

at the sawmill, a clipped twist
of barbed wire curled on the shoulder,
a screen door slamming

on the porch, a mockingbird roosting
in a butterfly bush & a black snake's
innards littered with feathers.

He's honeysuckle roping poison oak,
a gut-shot buck & cedar stump, an ax
abandoned in the creek bed's muck.

CURIOUS FACT

To furnish a mind,
make leaf-mold

from fecund matter
veining, branching,

a delicate way
to be conscious

of an actual leaf.
A charm of color,

Eastern Blue Star
& Milkweed,

the mental business
of decoration,

earthy, intricate
as Wood-Anemone.

LANDSCAPE WITH FOG

In the pasture, fog encircles a horse,
obscures muddy hooves.

*

Fog takes a bite of hay
& stands near a barbed-wire fence
that scrapes the underside
of every unfinished story.

*

A half-built house on the hill cannot breathe
when fog floats through soulless window holes.
A father with a rifle strides up the hill
& whispers to the fog: *Haunt me.*

*

In the woods, there's a deer stand
with no man sitting aimlessly inside it.
Deer saunter through the foggy field.
The father who built the stand
is where fog says he is.

*

Eventually, the sun is left
with the dirty work of dissipation.

*

Can you count the times fog
erased the landscape, enveloped
a father or a horse & never
gave them back?

*

Fog opens like a great white curtain
on the hillside & closes.

*

One morning a horse stood on the roadside.
His auburn mane flamed. The whites
of his eyes became inseparable from fog.
Blood stained his front legs.
The horse shimmered. He trembled.
Fog foretold his future.

                    *

Deer lie down in the pasture
near the half-built house. Their minds
are at ease.

                    *

And what of the father? Was his rifle
ever found?

FLOCK OF SWALLOWS

A necessary union: the farmhouse stood

beside the barn. Mama & I poured slop

in troughs, & Daddy's anger flew out of the structure's

mouth like a flock of swallows. *This goddamned thing*

won't start! he hollered. Over the tractor's sputters

& coughs, Mama called, *Wallace, please!* She pulled

me into her hip where flour from her apron

powdered my cheek. Grumbling from his seat,

Daddy coaxed the farm's surliest worker

until the motor caught & a shot of blurred

wings fluttered toward the field.

UNKEMPT PASTURE

Flurry of Tickseed,
Wingstem, Sneezeweed.

Jumble of rattleboxes
& insect hums. A tin

tub swirls with leaves.
Between fence posts

barbed wire droops.
The sun perks up.

The landscape's body
bristles with underbrush.

Lee's single-wide
sparkles nearby.

OCTOBER BEANS

To gaze at acres
of arable stars,

rummage
shimmering furrows,

pluck beans &
haul back buckets,

slide fingers
along pod seams,

feel a cross breeze
slip through

window screens
in Kathleen's kitchen.

To savor mouthfuls
of speckled clouds

picked from
just above ground

& sleep in the house
of late summer,

screen door
swollen on the porch.

CLOSER TO THE GROUND

Be in my mouth
        memory:
Eugene   Kathleen
a bucket   a spring
       a few pale leaves
& three acres of mud.
       As for me
cracks in walls   no furnace
       an old pot-bellied stove
& at dawn
haul water in hand.

ADOLPHUS' SCYTHE

Twisted vines the scythe whistle
thack whistle the scythe briars
in the mind the scythe whistle
thack the scythe in the thicket
whistle thack the scythe lopping
off the heads of purple thistles

Thistles of purple heads the off
lopping scythe the thack whistle
thicket in the scythe the thack
whistle scythe the mind in the
briars scythe the whistle thack
whistle scythe the vines unfisted

LITTLE SUMMER

after a line by Denis Johnson

God knows where, what kind of fire
blazed in the fox's eye,

what manner of farmer
crawled through a storm

to collapse at the back porch,
what sort of thorn poisoned

Ida's blood, & drowned summer
honeysuckle in a downpour.

God knows what type of lean-to
glimmered under its tin roof,

what turtle's shell scattered
on gravel & scorched shoulder.

God knows what fuss of wind
twisted weeds in soybeans.

He knows what barbs of wire
bristled in thunder's mouth.

God knows an ax blade stuck
in a stump, the eternal echo of rust.

BAND OF TAMBOURINES

There was a flutter
       in God's logic.

           A fisticuff & little
                 snort. One-two-

                three. One-two-
                      three. A rustling—

                      the shuffling sound
                            of hurried wings.

BROTHER BEEKEEPER

Herbert paid the Lord
in sweetness. Honey
dripped from his hands.

The Lord gave him grief
enough to feed the wind.
Herbert sheltered bees

in his pockets. He bumbled
up cemetery hill to shudder
beside his grieving kin.

The Lord has reasons,
his daddy cried. *The Lord
be damned,* his mama replied.

Every time they buried
one of his brothers, the bees'
sorrow flooded Herbert's head.

The ground made Thomas,
Walter, Louie, Henry & Roy,
a verdant bed.

WAKE

The front door opens
to a sleep box

where a boy rests
in a suit, shoes & socks.

He's a glum fellow
curl of cowlick

pallor of candlelight
ghosted in smoke.

This is to say
nothing of crows

or of Herbert eyeing
another brother's

soul slipping
down the road.

UNEXPECTED ATTRACTION

A five-gallon bucket
        dangles on a fencepost.

Raindrops echo. February
        shakes itself off, seeks

a dry spell. How long
        before winter yields?

In a flooded field
        a scarecrow on the ropes

entertains a black matter
        dressed in feathers.

II

FAMILY PORTRAIT

        i.

In a pasture littered
with muddy troughs

Daddy's voice calls,
Bring that bucket on!

A window looks out
on the field. The wind

tousles my thoughts.
On a rusted barb,

a burlap feed sack
snags & empties daylight.

        ii.

    Daddy's grandparents
    pose in porch chairs

    & between their feet rests
    a colander of peanut hulls.

    A boy eases forward
    to push open the screen door

    but the photographer stops
    his flight in black and white.

    There's no sign of future
    fatherhood in the boy's

    eyes, only a wish to run
    through the scene, to slosh

    through pastures
    & splash in the creek.

iii.

In my dreams, Daddy
glances at me.

His hand reaches back.
I withdraw.

His fingertips
are lit matchsticks

his voice buckshot
his love blackberries

nestled beneath a tangle
of roadside briars.

A HISTORY OF WIND

All we are is dust in
        The coat in the chair on the porch

                A boy's disheveled hair
                        Shimmer of flax in the pasture

                          A stallion's eyelashes
                                  The tin roof's curled corners

                                      Scattered leaves in the driveway
                        Sideways rain

                A snapped pine limb
              Curtains along the windowsills

    Ragged flag near the chicken houses
A bucket overturned in the field

WEATHER & JUG BAND

A sudden gust of loneliness
        in a glass jug. Beetles & slugs.

        Wind-bothered boughs pluck
                bedsprings, & in tin tubs,

                echoes of thunder.
        O scatter of rain tapping leaves.

        O hail rapping a rusted bucket.
Blues in late afternoon.

DEBRIS

Think of a father who slowly murders himself,
a booted farmer with crows at his feet & fate
on his breath like the scent of smoke & peppermint.

I don't miss him. Never have, but if I could
I'd pull back the curtain of death lingering
between our skins & ask him how he's been.

Daddy was a charge of lightning on my horizon.
He wept when I cracked my femur & scraped my knee
to bleeding, but his hands damaged me more
than any natural disaster. I'm debris

strewn across the pasture. I'm smoldering wood
& tin. My daddy was a meticulous twister
with fists. Don't touch me, lover. Don't touch me, friends.
Inherited weather seethes, storms, upends.

LAMP WICK

      Purple veins
in flicker
    of flame.
        Fever in scent
   of kerosene
    as rain
   picks up
in one room
      & finishes
        in another.
    Hot wick
  mimics
    the moon,
& in Lee's
  pasture
    a fleeing fox's
  ears prick
    midnight.
What prey
   trembles
     then slips
out of sight?

AMERICAN SENTENCES

Dianne's dead husband
tends the fields of her mind
every summer evening.

    *

Wallace's muscular back
& arms gleam like wet tin
in the afterlife.

    *

Sunlight & a bucketful
of rainwater scrub
Dianne's mind clean.

    *

On each cool morning, Wallace's
breath blurs the windows
of the old well house.

    *

The past is wood smoke
in a tangle of briars
& muscadines.

LANDSCAPE WITH RUINS

Two chimneys teeter in a scrub
of wild strawberries,

        & near the shell of a white farm truck,
        a baler rusts.

In a swath of sun, a lichen-covered
swing rocks.

        Ghost stories echo in the dirt parking lot
        of Teague's Farm & Market.

On the marquee: *De r corn*
& Pine Ne dles missing their e's.

TRACKS IN GRASS

i.

A bucket rolls
across the field
& a horse turns
his head.

Wind in bucket
bucket in wind
theme & variations
of handle & lid.

ii.

A slack line
of barbed
wire introduces
the flimsy idea
of boundaries.

In the horse's
mind, a door
swings open
& he saunters
into the dark.

WEATHER REPORT

When a traveling violinist
ambles through clouds at noon,
is it supper that she's wanting
or is her soul marooned?

Come on, the band leader cries,
incantations fill the air.
A line of cornetists
blast a thunderous fanfare.

A clarinetist shrieks.
Sax players honk their caws.
The sousaphonist oompahs
to the blacksmith's applause.

Old Reckless starts crowing
behind his mistress's house,
and the pond fills with tears
when his sadness tumbles out.

Dianne slams storm shutters.
Wallace threshes his crop,
and the mule bawls his troubles
till the tyrant's reins drop.

The parade keeps on rolling
bright on the landscape's rim.
The wind converts its malice
to a burst of gospel whim.

All the little saplings
whose limbs grow slick with pain
drop their flowery petals
and curled new leaves remain.

Play another number,
a tinny voice calls
from the farmhouse's kitchen,
with its grease-tainted walls.

BODY DOUBLE

Smoke drifted from a stove pipe while Mama stooped

washing beans in an iron vat. She was lusty

& dark & sparkled enough to have played Liz

Taylor's body double in *Cat on a Hot Tin Roof*,

that is if she hadn't inherited a plot

where she spent her summer mornings blanching corn

as steam dampened her skin. How many glances

out the window could I count if my small

shadow could return there now & watch her eyes

mull over the fields as my father plowed?

Was his muscled frame all that she could fathom,

but for a wasp clicking against the pane?

LANDSCAPE WITH TIME

When you get lost on the road, you run into the dead
wounded, smoke-eyed, wild
glittering with drops of rain.
For whatever blades, twigs, and mud,
bone of their bone,
dreams are reunions
blown by the lights of stars to the curling edge.

A few pale leaves appear
to be assembled again in the work room of the clouds.
Every star is sown; every field is blue.
It's like the floor of the sky fell out.

From what does not perish emerges what perishes
to the scrabble of claws, the fast treble in the chimney.
The world's changed: no angels at the top end now.
To navigate the dark you must listen,
see the white storm-brick wing across a breath of ash.

The room is emptier than nothingness.
The silver mirrors catch the bright stones and flares,
one hour again out of dark perpetuity.
Where is yesteryear's full moon that silvered?
Who grew and passed the almanac at night?

III

DISTANT RELATIONS

Where once a road cut through the woods to church,
the trees took over, making the route a vague
and winding sea of underbrush and junk:
a doorless fridge with leaves piled up inside,
one leather shoe, a heap of burned-out barrels.
All kinds of jars lie mired in the muck,
from large to small, stained coffee-brown, dark green
or clear. And on the mossy hilltop slope
there rests a rusted steel box frame, with springs
still twisted tight.

                        Jo Beth and Robert left
the pile right where their family farmhouse stood
until the night it burned. Robert's gone,
been dead for twenty years, and his widow's mind
has long been touched. She tries to call my name
when she's outside behind her double-wide
picking grapes. *Hello, hello*, she calls,
Honey, you want some grapes? They're sweet.
These grapes are mighty sweet.
I smile and walk away along the fence
past the tractor tires and bathroom sink.

THUNDER

In the summer dark, I stretched on a sleeper sofa

& listened as rain on tin told me stories.

The ways of husbands & wives astonished me.

In the back bedroom, my mother laid

with a man who would give her empty palms & pain

so vast she'd think the trees & fields had turned

their backs. A whippoorwill called out to the thunder.

Mice crawled inside the walls as Daddy's

moans trailed down the corridor. The stink

of mud & leaves drifted in through window screens.

PALE LIGHT

In the soul's
watery box,
a horse crouches.

His overcoat
reeks of smoke.
His pale light

glimmers
like a lantern
in the field.

The horse's
ribs rattle.
His eyes glance

deeper & deeper
into the storm.
In stable doors

fire flickers.
Singed hinges
whisper.

ASSEMBLAGES

after Thornton Dial, Sr.

I take a wheel, a shoe, a branch, a rope,

a piece of barbed wire, a broken lantern,

a milk bottle, a horse's skull, and hope

to make some sense of all these things, return

somethin' to earth. A man's inventions is

his life. The Lord laid out that kind of example

for man to go by, and so to me, it's His

Word that I'll follow. I can't go trample

on what the Lord done planned, and I don't care

what fall or what stand up 'cause life still goin'.

A man pick up some things. With Art, he dare

to make a record of what he got. Invention

is man's own knowledge tellin' him he fit

to find and build his life up bit by bit.

CHICKEN HOUSES

Smoke floats over the road
    while gloves gather reusable lumber.
        Laughter carries in the wind. Someone
            guns a salvage truck as others
                trudge over the ridge. They turn
            & a hand with three missing fingers
        waves. Who would believe me
    if I said none of us is made
of salvageable pieces? We come apart
        in the dark. Wood burns rain as leather faces
            fade. I glimpse only ghosts, not men.
                Wind repurposes them.

CLIMBING HYDRANGEA

To green

goes the glory

slipping upward,

winding

around silos

& signposts,

decorating

every upright

thing with fingers

of flourish, ebullient

vines weaving

through the mind

of a rusted machine

in the side yard,

seeking the divinity

of sun, of what was.

AGING FATHER

Don't smoke or drink,
eat less, the doctor urged him
but that advice, reiterated by his wife,

turned Daddy as ornery as the ass
that guarded the calves behind
the neighbor's noisy chicken houses.

Only at dusk when he perched
alone on the porch, smoking Old Golds
& petting his Lab, did he get a fleeting feeling

that he should give a damn. He watched
fireflies blink, go out, & he dropped
a half-smoked cigarette in his bourbon glass.

LANDSCAPE OF THE SPANGLED MIND

of OKRA
        on a roadside sign
of rainstorm
        in yesterday's corn
of junk pile
        & brushfire
of hog pen
        & frayed rope ends
of barn owl
        & muddy sow
of burlap sack
        & Ford tractor
of rusted gears
        & throats cleared
of arrowheads
        & collapsed sheds
of troubled sun
        & cow's skull
of jawbone
        crawling with bugs.

MIDDLE DISTANCE

Snowstorms cloud his mind's middle distance
& branches scrape the white barn's rusted roof.
In the pasture, Wallace repairs broken fences.
Snowstorms darken his mind's middle distance.

Newborn calves scatter. Wallace clenches
the wire. The night's no longer weatherproof.
Snowstorms howl in his mind's middle distance
& branches hammer the white barn's rusted roof.

INSTRUCTIONS FOR WINTER

The scent of kerosene drifts as a lantern is lit

& my father sits down at the kitchen table. Gunpowder

sparks on my tongue. The smell of metal coats

my teeth. My father's rifle stretches across

the table—we're halfway between hell & a clearing

in the woods. My father's sleeves hang threadbare

& bloody. His pale face & lips blaze.

This is a night of vines, of roadside thistles,

of an ashen man lit by a flame. A daughter

with a mouthful of rubble waits at the table,

& stares at a near-mirror image of herself.

PEERING THROUGH DECEMBER WINDOWS

A sudden crow flaps in from the south,
a black cloud filled with snow.

IN HIS MIND HE VIEWS A BLIZZARD

In a cinder block garden,
her father blooms in cold madness,
in a cuckoo room. Nurses shiver the man with no clothes.
The father who clashes with walls.
The father who lets language slip out of his grip.

*

Voices echo across the quarry. Trees shudder
as if mistaking themselves for ashen men.
Snow covers us up & Daddy drives through with no fear
of the road turning white on its axis & spinning us
into a ragged ditch.

*

In a blizzard we live, in a conflagration of evidence.
A red barn is our beacon before
our graves open & Daddy steps in. I follow
the road from snow to ash and back.

*

Daddy's supine with a mouth of garbled music,
a quarry of teeth & tongue
without so much as a *Goddamn,
look at me now*. His fingers chase
language like bird dogs sniffing for
scent. The cinder blocks blossom
& his daughter places a blessing in his ear.
Good thing death comes, she hums.

*

A world of disorder
freezes in Daddy's throat.
A ghost
rearranges himself
& loiters like a bluesman
with no way home.

PLOWMAN'S CHAPEL

Night's squeeze box—
every lit window
becomes a lantern
in a snowstorm.
A father's frame
flashes. A shadow
tangles his name.
Who's out back
snuggled in graves,
a flutter away
from the ruckus
of God's chorus
& one strong gust?

NOCTURNE

History
is a fistful
of feral weather,

a brief explosion
of snow.
Parts of us

litter
the roadside
where bare

vines climb
shafts
of moonlight

& faint
sounds of Coltrane
float above

a field
of felled stars.
Farmhouse

windows glow
like inextinguishable
lanterns.

An understory
of snow
cloaks the road.

A CERTAIN NOSTALGIA

Except for perhaps a cart horse
there is an empty place
some disjointed sentences,
a leaf, treeless.

Don't come any closer.
The birds spade the earth—
at once they return to floating.

The door is locked.
The water jug no longer freezes—
always slight variations
written on the belly of a crow.

SHADOWS KEEP HOUSE

The rusted
faucet
& its intermittent
drip
pings
in the porcelain sink
where Dianne's
rough hands
plunged
into the deep
of grease
& suds.

One blown lantern
rests
on the table
& in the chilled
night air
the breath
of a whippoorwill.

A ruddy road
slopes, &
in a field,
the echoing
yelp
of Daddy's bird dog.
In the glimmering air,
snowflakes
weave
a sweetness
through ghosts
& weeds.
Save me,
set me down
on a sunlit
path stirring
beneath
a dusting of clouds.

GOD IS PLENTY

& the wind wipes
the chimney's mouth

with a half gesture.
There is no rage,

only grief when bricks
twist away from

the farmhouse's frame.
Imagine the world

changes owners.
Blind-drunk fish

& forests take charge.
Stars crowd Mason jars.

Lightning bugs
prop up the dark.

ACKNOWLEDGMENTS

Thanks to the editors of the journals in which the following poems first appeared, sometimes in slightly different versions or with different titles:

"Departed Passing Through" published in *Blue Mountain Review*

"Landscape with Fog" published in *Interim: A Journal of Contemporary Poetry & Poetics*

"Flock of Swallows" published in *Nelle Literary Journal*

"Weather Report" published in *Measure: A Review of Formal Poetry*

"Body Double" published in *Nelle Literary Journal*

"Distant Relations" published in *Measure: A Review of Formal Poetry*

"Thunder" published in *Nelle Literary Journal*

"Assemblages" published in *Kweli Journal*

"Pale Light" and "Instructions for Winter" in *SWING Magazine*

A NOTE ON FORM

"A Landscape with Time" and "A Certain Nostalgia" are Centos— a poetic form composed entirely of lines from other works. This tradition dates back to antiquity, transforming existing language into new meaning through collage. These poems are woven from the words of a remarkable range of poets, and we gratefully acknowledge their original work.

"A Landscape with Time" — Frank Stanford, Stanley Kunitz Richard Wright, Wanda Coleman, Nicole Sealey, Raymond Patterson, Miller Williams, Deborah Digges, Carolyn Forche, Rob Shapiro, James Galvin, Alicia Ostriker, Ellen Bryant Voight, Richard Kenney, Rickey Laurentiis, Thomas Hardy, Wallace Stevens, Ezra Pound, Russell Atkins, Fred D'Aguiar, Nikki Finney.

"A Certain Nostalgia" — Primo Levi, Cesar Vallejo, Irena Klepfisz, Paul Celan, Claribel Alegria, Cristina Peri Rossi, Charles Simic, Nâzim Hikmet, Circe Maia, Adonis.

AUTHOR NOTE

I would like to thank Sarah Rose Nordgren and Charlotte Pence who provided guidance on this manuscript. Thanks also to Annie Woodford, Beth Copeland, David Masello, Lolita Stewart-White, Patricia Smith, and Susan Firer, poet-friends who always provide valuable feedback and support.

This book is dedicated to my mother, Dianne Whitehead, and my grandparents, Eugene and Kathleen Whitehead, who taught me how to respect and live in tandem with nature. I would also like to thank Kylee Carter, who brings to my life the awesome curiosity and creativity of a child.

PLAYLIST

To be listened to before, during, or after reading *Distant Relations*:

Natalie Merchant // *Spring and Fall: To A Young Child*

Kansas // *Dust in the Wind*

Frederic Chopin // *Nocturne, Opus posth. in C-sharp minor*

Franz Schubert // *Winterreise Die Krähe (The Crow)*

Benjamin Britten // *Serenade for Tenor, Horn, and Strings with Ian Bostridge*

Benjamin Britten // *Passacaglia & Four Sea Interludes: IV. Storm* from the opera, *Peter Grimes*

Peter Tchaikovsky // *Symphony #1 Winter Dreams*

Earl McDonald's Jug Band 1924-1927

Gustav Mahler // *Symphony No. 3: IVa. Sehr langsam. Misterioso. O Mensch! Gib acht! With Claudio Abbado and the Vienna Philharmonic, Jessye Norman*

Gustav Mahler // *Kindertotenlieder with Janet Baker*

Mahalia Jackson & Duke Ellington // *Keep Your Hand on The Plow with Mahalia Jackson and Duke Ellington*

Aretha Franklin (written by Donny Hathaway) // *Some Day We'll All Be Free*

Donny Hathaway // *Some Day We'll All Be Free*

John Coltrane // *A Love Supreme, Psalm*

Robert Schumann // *Dichterliebe im wunderschönen monat mai with Fritz Wunderlich*

LOBLOLLY PRESS

Loblolly Press is an independent press based out of Asheville, North Carolina that is dedicated to publishing contemporary poetry, short fiction, and novels from emerging and marginalized writers across the American South. Our goal is to publish writers with a distinctly Southern voice from communities and experiences not always represented in traditional publishing. We're striving to create a community of writers and readers who feel deeply connected to the work we publish because they can see themselves represented within it.

RECENT AND FORTHCOMING FROM LOBLOLLY PRESS

The Surfacing of Joy 🌰 Earl J. Wilcox (2023)

If Lost 🌰 Clint Bowman (2024)

Distant Relations 🌰 Cheryl Whitehead (2025)

The Computer Room 🌰 Emma Ensley (2025)

Habitats 🌰 Garrett Ashley (2026)

Book design and composition by Andrew Mack & Emma Ensley.
Editorial assistance from Eliza Alexander Wilcox.
Design assistance from Garrison Mack.

The headings and poems are set in Gellar and Cormorant.

www.ingramcontent.com/pod-product-compliance
Lightning Source LLC
Chambersburg PA
CBHW020603030426
42337CB00013B/1191